Jackie Robinson
He Was the First

A FIRST BIOGRAPHY

by David A. Adler

illustrated by Robert Casilla

HOLIDAY HOUSE / NEW YORK

IMPORTANT DATES

1919	Born January 31 near Cairo, Georgia.
1920	The Robinson family moved to California.
1939–1941	Starred on football, baseball, basketball and track teams at UCLA.
1942–1944	Served in U.S. Army.
1945	Played professional baseball on the Kansas City Monarchs of the Negro League.
1946	Played for the Montreal Royals.
1946	Married Rachel Isum, February 10.
1946	Son Jackie Jr. was born on November 18.
1947–1956	Played for the Brooklyn Dodgers.
1947	Named National League Rookie of the Year.
1949	Named National League Most Valuable Player.
1950	Daughter Sharon was born on January 13.
1952	Son David was born on May 14.
1957	Retired from baseball and began work for Chock Full O'Nuts.
1962	Elected to Baseball Hall of Fame.
1972	Died October 24 in Stamford, Connecticut.

CONTENTS

1. The Freedom Train

JACKIE ROBINSON was talented, determined and disciplined. He was a great athlete and a hero to baseball fans across the country. He was also a hero to supporters of equal rights for all people. In 1947, when he played for the Brooklyn Dodgers, he became the first black man to play modern-day major league baseball.

Jackie Robinson was born in a small, old farmhouse near Cairo, Georgia on January 31, 1919. Jackie's grandfather had been a slave. His father, Jerry Robinson, was a sharecropper and worked on a farm owned by someone else. Jerry Robinson kept half of what he grew. The owner of the farm kept the other half.

Mallie Robinson and her five children a few years after arriving in California. From left to right: Mack, Jack, Edgar, Mallie, Willa Mae, and Frank

Soon after Jackie was born, Jerry Robinson decided he was tired of farming. He said he might go as far away as Texas to look for some other kind of work. He left his wife Mallie and their five children in July 1919. He went off to Florida and never came back.

Without her husband to work the farm, Mallie Robinson and her children had to leave. They found a place to stay for awhile, but it was not a good time to be a black person in Georgia.

During the summer of 1919, there were terrible race riots in Chicago, Illinois, Elaine, Arkansas and in Washington D.C. There was trouble in Georgia, too. In April, black lodges and churches were burned in Millen, Georgia. A mob dragged a black prisoner from jail and killed him. In September, black schools in Georgia and more black churches were burned.

In May 1920, Mallie Robinson and her five children, carrying baskets, boxes, old suitcases, bags and bundles, headed West. Mallie called the train that took her family to California her ''Freedom Train.'' Jackie was just sixteen months old.

2. Pepper Street, Pasadena

WHEN THE Robinsons first came to California, they lived for awhile with Mallie's brother and his family. It was a crowded three-room apartment. There was no hot water. They took baths in the same metal tub they used to clean pots and dishes. Jackie's mother left the apartment early each morning to work as a laundress, washing and ironing clothes.

The Robinsons had been poor in Georgia, and they were poor in California. Sometimes there wasn't enough money to buy food for three meals a day. Often the meals they ate were day-old bread and sweet water, water with sugar added to it.

A few years later, the Robinsons moved to a house on 121 Pepper Street in Pasadena. They were the only black family on the block. Many of their neighbors were not happy to have them there. They called the Robinson children ugly names. They held meetings and signed petitions to get them to move. Someone even burned a cross on the front lawn to frighten Mallie and her children. But Mallie Robinson would not move.

Jackie was proud and stubborn, too, just like his mother. When he was about eight years old, one of the neighbor's children yelled at him. Jackie yelled right back. The girl's father came out of the house, and soon the man and Jackie were throwing stones at each other. The fight ended when the man's wife came outside and told him not to fight with a child.

Jackie was just four years old when his family moved to Pepper Street. He was too young to go to school but there was no one to stay at home with him. His mother went to work every day. So Jackie went to school with his sister, Willa Mae. Jackie sat outside and played in the sandbox while she was in class. When it rained, Willa Mae's teachers rushed to bring Jackie in with the other children. At the end of the school day, Willa Mae took him home.

Black children were not treated as equal citizens in Pasadena, and Jackie knew it. They were allowed in the public swimming pool only one day a week, Tuesday. In movie theaters, they were allowed to sit only in the balconies. Mallie Robinson told her children not to cause trouble. But she also taught them not to run away from a problem. She taught them to be proud, that they were as good as anyone.

3. The Young Athlete

JACKIE LOVED to play outside. When he was just a few years old, his mother made a ball for him by wrapping a rag around the wool from an old sock. Jackie loved to throw that rag ball up and catch it. He did that again and again. He was good at it. And Jackie practiced hitting the rag ball with a stick. He was good at that, too.

In school, there were two baseball teams that played at recess and during lunch. Both teams wanted Jackie. It was easy for Jackie to decide which team to join. The players on one team offered to share their lunches with Jackie if he would play on their team. Jackie saved his mother the expense of giving him lunch. He had plenty to eat. And he played baseball.

Jackie was proud that he was able to save his mother some money. He was even prouder when he was able to earn a dollar or two to give to her. Jackie did errands, mowed lawns and sold newspapers to earn money. He wrote later that as a boy his proudest moments were when he was able to help his mother in that way.

But there were moments he would remember without pride. When Jackie was older, he and a rough group of friends all belonged to the Pepper Street gang. It was not a violent gang, but the boys did get into plenty of trouble. They threw clods of dirt at passing cars, even at police cars. Then they ran off to hide. They stole fruit. They hid behind trees at a local golf course and when a ball landed nearby, they took it. Then they waited, watched and laughed as the golfer searched for the ball. Later the boys sold the golf balls to other golfers. Sometimes the boys got away with their pranks. Many times they were caught and taken to the police station.

Carl Anderson worked nearby and watched Jackie and the Pepper Street gang. He told Jackie that he didn't belong in a gang. He said that Jackie hurt his mother when he got into trouble. And Carl Anderson said it would take courage for Jackie to leave the gang.

Jackie had courage. He left the gang and spent much of his extra free time at the church. The new minister had set up sports programs and dances for the young people. Later, when Jackie was in college, he taught Sunday school at the same church.

At John Muir Technical High School, Jackie was just an average student, but he was an outstanding athlete. He was on the baseball, football, basketball and track teams. He was quick, determined and very competitive. He was a team leader. Opposing players and coaches knew that if they could stop Robinson, they could beat the John Muir team. They tried to upset Jackie, to get him angry and forget about the game by making racial remarks. Their remarks only made Jackie more determined to win.

Jackie at bat as a young man

Most times, when Jackie played, his brother Frank was in the stands watching, cheering and hollering advice. Frank was Jackie's greatest fan. He felt Jackie was as good as any player anywhere.

Frank was disappointed when Jackie wasn't offered an athletic scholarship by a major university. After Jackie graduated from high school, he went to a local school, Pasadena Junior College.

Jackie wasn't the first Robinson at Pasadena Junior College. His brother Mack had gone there, too. Mack was a hero to Jackie and to many of the students at the college. Mack had competed in the 1936 Olympics in Berlin, Germany. He finished second to the great Jesse Owens in the 2,000-meter race. Mack had won a silver medal.

Jackie was a star athlete at Pasadena Junior College, too. Jackie was quarterback for the football team. He was the basketball team's top scorer. He was also on the track and baseball teams.

Jackie's greatest day in Junior College sports was in May 1938. In the morning, Jackie competed in a track meet in Pomona, California and set a new Junior College running broad jump record. Jackie's friend was sitting in a car waiting for him.

Jackie ran to the car, and they drove off to Glendale where he played shortstop for the Pasadena team.

That day, the baseball team won the league championship. Jackie was voted the most valuable junior college baseball player in southern California.

Pasadena was a two-year college. When Jackie graduated, he was offered scholarships to some fine universities. But Jackie decided to go to nearby UCLA, so he could live at home, and so his brother Frank could still watch him play.

But Frank never saw Jackie play for UCLA. Frank died in May 1939 of injuries from a motorcycle accident. It was a terrible loss for Jackie.

4. College Hero

AT UCLA Jackie was the first student to win a letter in four sports. He starred in baseball and track. He was the top scorer on the basketball team, the top scorer in the entire division. But it was in football that Jackie became the campus hero. He and another black player, Kenny Washington, were the team's stars.

During the 1939 college football season, UCLA was a surprise to many football fans. The team didn't lose all year, although three games did end in a tie. In the second game of the season, Jackie ran sixty-five yards for the winning touchdown. In another game, Jackie caught a forty-three-yard pass and ran another twenty-three yards for a touchdown. Later in the same game, he ran more than eighty yards for still another touchdown. In game after game, thousands of fans stood and cheered for Jackie Robinson, Kenny Washington and their teammates.

Jackie was a hero to most of his UCLA classmates. But to Rachel Isum, a first-year nursing student who watched Jackie stand on the football field with his hands on his hips, he was cocky, conceited.

One day Jackie's friend introduced him to Rachel. She was beautiful, intelligent and warm. Jackie especially liked her honesty. He felt he could tell her anything, and she would understand. And Rachel discovered that Jackie wasn't conceited at all. He was somewhat shy.

In 1941, shortly before he was to graduate from college, Jackie left school. He was impatient. He wanted to earn money to help his mother.

Jackie's first job after he left school was as the assistant athletic director at a camp for underprivileged children. But the camp was closed soon after Jackie started working.

Jackie went to Honolulu, Hawaii. He worked for a construction company and on Sundays, he played football for the Honolulu Bears. It was a professional team. They paid him to play.

While Jackie was in Hawaii, there was terrible trouble elsewhere in the world. Thousands of miles away, in Europe, there was war.

On December 7, 1941 the Japanese bombed Pearl Harbor, Hawaii. Jackie Robinson was already on a ship on his way back home. The ship was in danger of being attacked. Crew members blackened the portholes of the ship so that at night its lights wouldn't be seen. By the time Jackie reached California, the United States was at war.

5. Army Life

EARLY IN 1942 Jackie Robinson was drafted to serve in the United States Army. He was sent to Fort Riley, Kansas. After he completed basic training, Jackie applied for Officers' Candidate School. He passed all the entrance tests, and then he waited. The other black soldiers who had applied with Jackie waited, too. But white soldiers who applied at the same time were already in the school.

A few months later Sergeant Joe Louis, a black and the heavyweight boxing champion of the world, was sent to Fort Riley. Jackie told him what was happening. Soon after that, Jackie and the other black soldiers were allowed into the school. Jackie rose to the rank of second lieutenant.

Jackie was transferred to Fort Hood, Texas. While he was there, riding on an army bus, he was told to get up and sit in the back where he belonged. Blacks throughout the South were sent to the backs of buses. But this was the army and such segregation was not allowed. Jackie didn't move.

When Jackie got off the bus, he was met by the military police. He was brought before an army captain. They argued.

Jackie was court-martialed, put on trial by the army. He was accused of not showing proper respect for a superior officer and for disobeying orders. He was judged to be innocent.

After the court-martial, Jackie asked to be released from the army. He was sent to Camp Breckinridge, Kentucky where he waited for his discharge papers. While he was there, he met another black soldier who had been a pitcher for the Kansas City Monarchs, a professional black baseball team. He told Jackie to write to the owner of the team. Jackie wrote the letter and in April 1945, he joined the team. He had a new job now. He was being paid to play baseball.

6. A Ballplayer with Guts

PROFESSIONAL BASEBALL in 1945 was a segregated sport. Only whites played on the major league teams. Blacks played in the Negro Leagues on such teams as the Kansas City Monarchs, Homestead Grays, Pittsburgh Crawfords and the Birmingham Black Barons.

There were a few protests in the 1940s by some politicians and newsmen. Some people stood outside baseball stadiums carrying signs. They argued that black soldiers had fought and some had died for America. They should be able to play baseball, too.

During the 1945 baseball season, Jackie played shortstop for the Kansas City Monarchs. While he was playing, scouts for the Brooklyn Dodgers, an all-white major league baseball team, were watching him and other black ballplayers. Branch Rickey, the president of the Brooklyn Dodgers, had decided it was time to end segregation in baseball.

The Brooklyn Dodger scouts wrote reports on many of the stars in the Negro leagues. Branch Rickey was looking for a good black ballplayer with the courage to be the first black player in modern major league baseball. After reading the reports of his scouts, he chose Jackie Robinson.

Branch Rickey asked Jackie if had the guts to play white baseball. Could he look away when people would call him ugly names? Could he walk away when players on other teams would purposely try to injure him?

"Mr. Rickey," Jackie asked, "are you looking for a Negro who is afraid to fight back?"

That wasn't what Branch Rickey was looking for at all. He told Jackie Robinson, "I'm looking for a ballplayer with guts enough *not* to fight back."

In October 1945, Jackie Robinson signed a contract to join the Montreal Royals, the top minor league team of the Brooklyn Dodgers. He would play there for a year and then join the Dodgers. Jackie was given a bonus and would get a good salary. Jackie had enough money to think about marriage.

Jackie and Rachel Isum had dated, written to each other and spoken on the telephone ever since they met at UCLA in 1940. On February 10, 1946 they were married in a big church wedding in California. Rachel was a real helpmate for Jackie. Having her with him made the next few difficult years a little easier.

From left to right: Royals' president Hector Racine,
Branch Rickey, Jackie, and Royals' vice president
J. Romeo Gauvreau, as Jackie signs the Montreal Royals
contract

Branch Rickey had been right. During the 1946 baseball season, fans and players did call Jackie Robinson ugly names. In some cities in Florida, during spring training, games were canceled because it was against the law for a black to play on the same field with whites. In some cities Jackie and Rachel could not stay at the hotel with the other players. And they could not get served in many restaurants. During a game in Syracuse, New York, the players on the other team threw a black cat onto the field and yelled "Hey, Jackie, there's your cousin."

Jackie Robinson was a talented athlete. The ugly names people called him and the hotels that wouldn't let him in only made Jackie more determined to play his best.

Wherever the Montreal Royals played, thousands of people came to watch. Many of the fans were black people. In some stadiums, black fans were allowed to sit only in certain sections. But thousands came anyway, just to see Jackie.

In 1946 Jackie Robinson and the Montreal Royals did not disappoint their fans. Jackie was the top batter in the league. The Montreal Royals won the pennant and the Little World Series. In 1946 they were the top minor league team in baseball.

After the final game of the season, Jackie returned to the clubhouse. Before he could change out of his baseball uniform, a stadium usher told Jackie that the fans wanted to see him to say good-bye. Jackie went outside. Thousands of fans were waiting for him. They shook his hand. They hugged and kissed him. They carried Jackie on their shoulders. He was their hero.

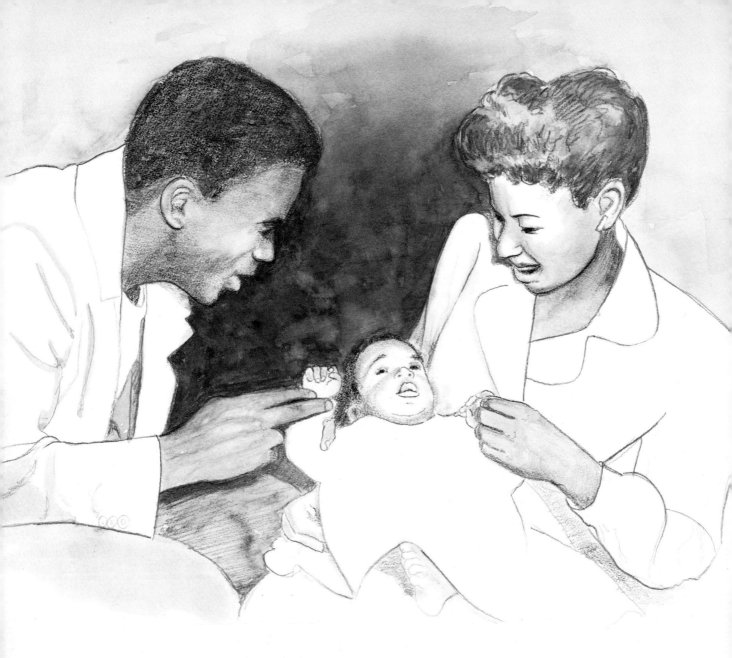

There was more good news in 1946. In November, Rachel
and Jackie Robinson had their first child, a son. They named
him Jackie, Jr.

In the spring of 1947, the Montreal Royals and the Brooklyn
Dodgers trained in Havana, Cuba. Jackie trained with the
Royals. He hoped that before the regular season began he would
join the Dodgers.

On April 10, 1947 newsmen were handed a printed statement signed by Branch Rickey. *The Brooklyn Dodgers today purchased the contract of Jack Roosevelt Robinson from Montreal. He will report immediately.*

Jackie and Branch Rickey

7. Jackie Was the First

BEING THE first black player wasn't easy. Jackie got plenty of hate mail. There were threats that Jackie and his wife would be shot, that their son would be kidnapped.

During a series of games early in the season against the Philadelphia Phillies, a few players and the manager of the Phillies were especially cruel. They yelled horrible things at Jackie and at his teammates. They held their bats like rifles, made gunshot noises and laughed. Jackie was angry. He wanted to run into the Phillies' dugout and fight. But he didn't.

In Cincinnati the fans and the players on the other team yelled at Jackie and at his teammate, Pee Wee Reese. Pee Wee answered them all. He put his arm around Jackie and let everyone know that they were friends. That meant a lot to Jackie.

From left to right: Rick Bridges, Bud Podbielan, Jackie, Pee Wee Reese, and Rube Walker

During the first few games of the season, Jackie had trouble hitting. He made an error in the field, and the Dodgers almost lost the game. But then Jackie began to hit and field the way he had in Montreal.

Nineteen forty-seven was a good year in baseball for Jackie Robinson. Jackie played in almost every game that year. He had 175 hits, including twelve home runs. He scored 125 times, led the league in stolen bases and was selected as the Rookie of the Year.

Nineteen forty-seven was also a good year for the Brooklyn Dodgers. They won the National League pennant. They played

the New York Yankees—the American League winners—in the World Series. The Yankees won, four games to three.

In 1949, Jackie had his best season in baseball. He had the highest batting average in the National League, .342, and the most stolen bases. Of the 200 players in the league, Jackie was voted the best, the National League's Most Valuable Player.

The Dodgers won the pennant in 1949, too. But again they lost the World Series to the New York Yankees.

After winning the World Series

While Jackie Robinson played for the Dodgers, the team won six pennants, in 1947, 1949, 1952, 1953, 1955, and 1956. All six times they played against the Yankees in the World Series. They won in 1955 and were the world champions of baseball. Jackie considered winning the World Series one of the greatest thrills of his life.

Jackie played baseball until the end of the 1956 season. During his years with the Dodgers, many other blacks joined major league teams including Roy Campanella, Don Newcombe, Larry Doby, Satchel Paige, Ernie Banks, Monte Irvin, Willie Mays and Hank Aaron. They were all great players, but Jackie was the first.

8. Triumph and Tragedy

AFTER THE 1956 season, the new president of the Dodgers traded Jackie to the New York Giants. But Jackie never played for them. At thirty-seven he was old for a baseball player, and not as quick as he had been just a few years before. Even before the trade was announced, he had decided to retire from baseball and take a job offered to him by the Chock Full O'Nuts restaurants.

Jackie was busy in the years following his retirement from baseball. He became an active leader in the Civil Rights movement. He made speeches, spoke with political leaders and marched to gain equal rights for blacks. He helped to establish the Freedom National Bank in Harlem, New York. And after he left Chock Full O'Nuts, he became a special assistant to Governor Nelson Rockefeller of New York.

Jackie was also busy with his family. After Jackie Jr. was born, Jackie and Rachel had two more children. Sharon was born in 1950 and David in 1952.

From left to right: Rachel, David,
Sharon, Jackie Jr., and Jackie

JACK R ROOSEVELT ROBINSON

BROOKLYN N.L. 1947 TO 1956

LEADING N.L. BATTER IN 1949 HOLDS
FIELDING MARK FOR SECOND BASEMAN
PLAYING IN 150 OR MORE GAMES WITH .992
LEAD N.L. IN STOLEN BASES IN 1947 AND
1949 MOST VALUABLE PLAYER IN 1949
LIFETIME BATTING AVERAGE .311 JOINT
RECORD HOLDER FOR MOST DOUBLE PLAY
BY SECOND BASEMAN 137 IN 1951
LED SECOND BASEMEN IN DOUBLE
PLAYS 1949 50 51 52

Perhaps the highlight of the years following Jackie's retirement from baseball was his election to the Baseball Hall of Fame in 1962.

Jackie spoke briefly at the ceremony. He said "I feel quite inadequate to this honor. It is something that could never have happened without three people, Branch Rickey was as a father to me, my wife and my mother. They are here making the honor complete."

Afterwards, fans crowded around Jackie Robinson and the three other new Hall of Famers. Jackie took pictures of it all with his home movie camera. He wanted to remember that moment.

Being elected to the Hall of Fame was a great triumph for Jackie Robinson. But along with the work, his civil rights' and political activities, and the honors, there was tragedy in Jackie's life. In 1965 Branch Rickey died. Three years later Mallie Robinson, Jackie's mother, died. That same year, 1968, Jackie Jr. was arrested for possessing illegal drugs.

Jackie Jr. sought help and ended his need for drugs. He worked to help others with similar problems. Then in June, 1971, Jackie Jr. was driving to his parent's home when his car skidded and crashed. Jackie Jr. was killed.

Jackie Robinson's health was also a problem. He had diabetes and heart disease. He was just fifty years old when he began to lose his sight. He died of a heart attack on October 24, 1972. Jackie Robinson was just fifty-three years old.

Because Jackie Robinson was so good in so many sports, he is considered to have been one of America's greatest athletes. As a baseball player he was a great fielder, a powerful hitter and a daring, exciting base runner. But he is remembered as much for his courage as for his talents as an athlete. His appearance in a Dodger uniform in a major league baseball game was a major event in the movement toward equal rights for all Americans. Today millions of children dream of one day playing major league baseball. That dream was made possible for black children by Jackie Robinson.

INDEX

To a great baseball fan and a good friend, ALICE BELGRAY

Text copyright © 1989 by David A. Adler
Illustrations copyright © 1989 by Holiday House, Inc.
All rights reserved
Printed in the United States of America

LIBRARY OF CONGRESS CATALOGING-IN-PUBLICATION DATA

Adler, David A.
Jackie Robinson: he was the first / written by David A. Adler:
illustrated by Robert Casilla. — 1st ed.
p.   cm.
Includes index.
Summary: Traces the life of the talented and determined athlete
who broke the color barrier in major league baseball in 1947 by
joining the Brooklyn Dodgers.
ISBN 0-8234-0734-9
1. Robinson, Jackie, 1919-1972—Juvenile literature. 2. Baseball
players—United States—Biography—Juvenile literature.
[1. Robinson, Jackie, 1919-1972.   2. Baseball players.   3. Afro-
Americans—Biography.]   I. Casilla, Robert, ill.   II. Title.
GV865.A37 1989
796.357'092'4—dc 19
[B]   88-23294   CIP   AC

ISBN 0-8234-0734-9
ISBN 0-8234-0799-3 (pbk.)